£1.99

G000123102

ISLAND C]

This book has been published with generous financial support from the following local businesses, for which the editor and publishers would like to express their sincere thanks:

The Elm Tree, Cowley Road
Flanagan Teasdale, Solrs, Summertown
Gill & Co. (Ironmongers), High Street
D. L. Harris, Dental Surgeon, Summertown
Jude the Obscure, Walton Street
The Old Tom, St Aldates
River Racing, Kingston Road

Island City

Oxford poems by living Oxford poets

chosen and introduced by

Rip Bulkeley

Broad Street Poetry

1999

Acknowledgements

The editor and publishers wish to thank Carcanet Press Ltd and Anne Ridler for permission to reprint "Snakeshead Fritillaries" from her *Collected Poems*, 1994; Carcanet Press Ltd and Jon Stallworthy, for permission to reprint "The Almond Tree" and "Poem upon the Quincentenary of Magdalen College" from his *Rounding the Horn: Collected Poems*, 1998; Peterloo Poets and Olivia Byard, for permission to reprint "Scotland in an Oxford Landscape" from her collection *From a Benediction*, 1998; Picador, an imprint of Macmillan Publishing Ltd (in association with the Salisbury Festival) and Kate Clanchy, for permission to reprint her poem "Feller, Son & Daughter" from the collection *Last Words: new poetry for the new century*, 1999; and Salzburg Poetry and Anne Born, for permission to print a new version of her poem "Ox Carts at the Ford", which first appeared in *Histories*, by Anne Born and Alex Smith, 1998. Kathleen McPhilemy's "Avoiding the Cracks", from her collection *A Tented Peace*, Katabasis, 1995, and Jamie McKendrick's "The Century Plant", from his collection *The Marble Fly*, Oxford University Press, 1997, are works in which the rights have been retained by or reverted to the authors. An earlier version of Polly Clark's "Sunset over Port Meadow" was published by *Thumbscrew*, and this new version will appear in her forthcoming collection *Kiss*, to be published by Bloodaxe in 2000.

The outline of Oxford's rivers and streams, used on the cover, was prepared by Clare Pope on the basis of the Ordnance Survey's 1919 and 1922 6-inch map series for Oxfordshire and Berkshire. The street map used for in-text decorations was published *c*.1955 by the former Sun Map Co. of Dunstable.

Copyright

Introduction and "The Saxon Pin" © 1999, 1998 Rip Bulkeley. All rights in all other poems published here remain either with their authors or with their previous publishers under existing contractual arrangements, and no correspondence about their further publication will be entered into by Broad Street Poetry.

Orders

This book can be purchased only from bookshops and other retail outlets in Oxford or else by direct mail-order from within the United Kingdom at £7 a copy. Sterling cheques should be made out to 'Rip Bulkeley' and sent to the address below. Overseas and postal bookshop orders cannot be accepted.

First published in 1999
by Broad Street Poetry
38 Lonsdale Road, Oxford, OX2 7EW, U.K.

ISBN 0-9537126-0-5

Designed by Oxford Designers & Illustrators
Printed in Great Britain by Information Press, Oxford

£1.99
wk
fc

"This Oxford ... is surrounded with more clear streams than I ever saw together. I take a walk by the side of one of them every evening."

John Keats, writing to his sister Fanny
10 September 1817

Contents

Introduction

This book was conceived as a collection of shortish poems set in Oxford and written by people who live or work in Oxford today. I had always planned to stretch that concept slightly to include a piece by the late Sally Horsman, a fine young poet and member of the *Last Gasp* writers group, who was killed in an air crash two years ago. But along the way the limits of 'Oxford' and of the other elements of the definition were also challenged, beneficially in most cases. The end result remains fairly close to the original idea.

In Oxford as elsewhere, people who write poems have widely differing uses for what they are doing, as well as skills and experience in the art. While seeking and often thankfully receiving the best from the best, I have been conscious that so-called 'lesser' pieces could also contribute something worthwhile to the collection as a whole. Had it been confined to (someone's definition of) very good poems, the overall portrait of Oxford would have suffered considerably. Instead I hope that, by varying the literary level or intensity of its contents, the book may prove palatable to readers who care for Oxford at least as much as, perhaps more than, they care for poetry.

Even so, it was not possible to accept contributions from all the 77 people who offered them. In the difficult task of selection, I am much beholden to the six poets who met at my house one Sunday in July to look over some of the submissions, and who have rightly chosen to remain anonymous. I may sometimes have bent or strayed from their recommendations, from anthological motives. But in most cases I have gratefully followed their advice. To those whose poems were not included, let me repeat my thanks for having been allowed to see them.

I have tried to represent the wide range of poetries that are active in our city. But comparison of this collection with other Oxford anthologies of the past decade reveals that my success has been partial at best. Some of those approached regretted that they had nothing suitable to offer me. Others, quite understandably, did not reply. But at least some of the noticeable absences must be attributed to my imperfect knowledge of Oxford's fragmented poetry scene and my inadequate publicization of the project, assisted though I often was by the suggestions or the word of mouth of contributors. All the same, I hope there are at least a few strange bed-fellows within these pages. And if any reader (one rather saintly friend excepted) likes every poem, I shall be disappointed.

As they finally are, the poets have been presented only through their poems, without details of their lives or literary achievements. Several have national or international reputations. Their names will speak for them, and will also testify to the generosity of their unpaid contributions. (I probably should add, for a few readers, that the people with more than one poem in the book were by no means selected as better or more important than their colleagues.)

Any anthology devoted to a single place is likely to contain variations on certain shared themes, the largest and most fitting of which, in the present case, is Oxford's many-sided history. Fritillaries, streams, water-birds, street people, Port Meadow, even the long-debated ford itself, are amongst those features which appear more than once. However, they play different roles in very different poems. But this is no guide book, and other familiar landmarks, from the Rover Works to the Playhouse or the ice rink, do not happen to be addressed. Sexual love, that time-honoured poetic opportunity, is scarce, and when it does crop up the sexuality is sometimes more evident than the love. Religious belief is at least as prominent an aspect of life in these pages. One striking characteristic shared by almost but not quite all the poems is the absence of the poet's own work-place. But these are probably general signs of the poetic times, rather than attributes peculiar to Oxford.

The order in which the poems have been placed, with minor deviations imposed by the demands of book design, is that of a right-handed spiral, moving out from the neigh-bourhood of Magdalen Bridge, the central buckle of our two-fold city. Poems which are not located precisely enough for such a determination, and which therefore have no (sometimes redundant) place-names beside them, have been inserted at considered intervals.

And why *Island City*? I first applied the phrase to Oxford in a recent poem, not included here. But its seeds were planted forty years ago, when I read a book about Oxford town planning which emphasized that the city's survival depended on the upstream control of the Thames and the Cherwell, and explained that the relative inaccessibility of its gravel peninsula, surrounded by marshy flood-plains, had been responsible for the neglect of the site by the Romans and thus for its late settlement by comparison with nearby Abingdon and Dorchester. Since then I have learned that poets and other writers have long celebrated Oxford's special character as a city lapped and threaded by many waters, some of which are now hidden from view. And of course the phrase also bears other readings.

Besides the informal editorial panel, mentioned above, many people have generously helped to make this book. Noel Reilly, publican of the *Jude the Obscure* in Walton Street, was at all times a source of good advice and optimistic com-mon sense. The *Poetic Licence* group lent me their contacts list. Clare Pope produced the map of Oxford rivers used on the cover. Oxford Designers & Illustrators worked wonders to lift the project out of the muddle of desk-top publishing and into the sadly diminishing sphere of real books. Greg

3

Sweetnam contributed valuable advice on the production process. The sponsors, listed elsewhere, are local firms which had the vision to respond positively to a vague description of an incomplete project from an unknown petitioner. My wife Jane has provided constant and much needed support. To all these my heartfelt thanks.

It remains for me to thank what is at least a large contingent of the poets of Oxford, for the poems they allowed me to choose from and then to publish without fees, for their useful advice, and for the tolerance and good humour with which they handled my often misconceived or poorly worded attempts to develop the skills of anthologist and editor as I went along. This book was, obviously, created by them, with only the smallest help from me. I hope that they, and their fellow-citizens, and some of the many guests whom our city welcomes every year, will find plenty to recognize (warts and all) and to enjoy in the pages which follow.

RIP BULKELEY
September 1999

Snakeshead Fritillaries

Some seedlings shoulder the earth away
Like Milton's lion plunging to get free,
Demanding notice. Delicate rare fritillary,
You enter creeping, like the snake
You're named for, and lay your ear to the ground.
The soundless signal comes, to arch the neck –
Losing the trampled look –
Follow the code for colour, whether
White or freckled with purple and pale,
A chequered dice-box tilted over the soil,
The yellow dice held at the base.

When light slants before the sunset, this is
The proper time to watch fritillaries.
They entered creeping; you go on your knees,
The flowers level with your eyes,
And catch the dapple of sunlight through the petals.

ANNE RIDLER

Oxford Water

for Brendan

Michaelmas rain makes
craters of the moon
on the surface of the Thames.

Barges dark against brooding,
blond-black, midwinter canal:
Jericho murders.

A tarmac-banked, London-bent,
modern river cold-shoulders
the Wharf House.

Saxon streams capillary
under concrete:
alternative Oxford.

Hilary rainfall: pieces
of broken mirror
along the towpath.

Russet-cream cattle look on
as a quiet lake invades
a meadow.

White lilies float on a circle
of stone-bound water:
Hermes commands.

Green water drips down
a concrete, Jacobson wall:
Virginia creeper.

A solitary canoe silver-arrows
across the Cherwell:
finals.

Castle Mill Stream slips past
industrial obsolescence
to freedom.

MARGARET CLERICI

The Century Plant

A century after its introduction
to Oxford's Botanic Gardens greenhouse,
on the site of the medieval Jewish cemetery,
the agave has taken a leap of faith
it won't survive, and begun to blaze
with sulphurous buds. It's not clear whether
global or more local warming lit the fuse
in the patient rootstock and sent one limb
rocketing upward so its top
can look down even on the banana tree
besides the other transplants. The palm-line
is said to move a metre north each year
– these days more like a kilometre –
but either way the agave's too far ahead
to be caught up with, despite the hundred years
of waiting – now two, at the most three weeks
of prodigal flowering and the whole thing ends.

In 1850 in Seville,
while his contemporaries photographed
rotting barges on the Guadalquivir
or farm labourers in sheepskin waistcoats
or Gypsy women in the tobacco factory,
Vicomte J. de Vigier
turned his back on the folkloric and his lens
on the common-or-garden naturalized exotics
like palm trees and bamboo. His masterpiece,
Etude d'aloès, shows this tumid
dusty plant on a nondescript roadside.

It holds grimly on to its patch of nowhere
and drinks and drinks the silver nitrate light
as though there were no belonging anywhere
but there and then, and nothing sublime
except that stretch of dirt, that broken wall
and the rays of a faded nineteenth-century sun.

JAMIE MCKENDRICK

Poem upon the Quincentenary of Magdalen College

The chapel silent and the candles weeping.
White boys erect, each with the sun
alive beneath his skin and gold blood leaping,
stooped in one hour; were levelled soon
with the arterial weeping of despair
into old men. Although a lifetime slips
through this night's sorrow, none will shift his stare.
Their beards shake white below the fluttering lips,
their hands still tremble in the stress of prayer.

They weep because no guests will mourn with them
the dying of five hundred Junes.
Tongued bells are dumb: the requiem
sleeps in the organ's throat, and tunes
swirl only on the tented lawn. No psalms
are scrolled in smoke above the shadow pall,
but for this night, freed from a mason's charms,
the stone musicians tip-toe from the wall
with tabret, lute and viol in their arms.

For one not lit with eyes the pipers blow
nothing but silver, fiddlers weave
a tent of scarlet with the shuttle bow.
What more should he believe
beyond the kiss of taffeta and shower
of heels? Like shells that toll for their bell-tongued seas
his ears ring back the changes of the hour.
He only understands the prophecies
of iron pigeons gathering in the tower.

It seemed he whistled as the night was failing
a dirge for unremembered years,
and on his face the moth-winged rain was falling
persistent as the candles' tears;
and neither priest nor prophet turned his head
for whirling girls or laughter from the crowd.
These saw the Great Tower gilded: they instead,
through the sarcophagus, through mask and shroud,
saw naked the dimensions of the dead.

Now morning shovels in the sunlight, bringing
a blackbird in the last tail-coat
to raise the requiem. He stills us, singing
in the small chantry of his throat
the song the blind boy whistled through the rain.
The dancers all have dwindled into stone,
the mourners given up their ghosts of flame.
Tabret and lute and kettle-drum alone
in carven hands upon the arch remain.

JON STALLWORTHY

By Bat-Willow

Normally, the snow-drops are an ordered bunch.
Not martial, but decorative and still
Like the tasselled fringe of an altar-cloth
Or the lilies carved on the chapel wall.
I come about this time, most years,
To see that they have made a showing
Of getting on with the business of spring.
But this year they seem to be slipping onto the path
As if to buttonhole the passers-by.
Scattered and unruly, they eye off and laugh
At cattle stood in the water meadow
Who return a stare, ageless and wise.
And I think this is my idea of paradise:
The grass grown tufty and uneven
The trees quite unashamedly bare
An unseasonal dusting of sparrows
The daffodils not yet fully aware.
But more than this is the implication
Of always something more to come;
The intent of an unpretentious path
Always leading through or from
A ragged kind of Heaven.

J. M. BAILEY

Scotland in an Oxford Landscape

The stream's tidy banks have fled,
routed, when the river took the borderland
and lost its own identity. Isolated trees
mark mere possibilities, as if this were
a medieval map, where stained brown outlines
suggest the edge of a world which has been
heard of but not yet visited. Dabchicks
drift nodding on the current between,
as though the trunks were supports
for toppled dolmens and they sounded ley lines
like diviners. Beneath, lies debris:
the small river animals' habitats, voles,
otters, rats, avenues of spring anemones,
and tiny wild crocuses that smudge your eyesight
briefly, with enigmatic purple. Treasure,
to be found again, of a more bucolic Atlantis.

OLIVIA BYARD

i. m.

He pitched his tent by the river
at Osney; warmed himself in corners
of bars, bothering no one. Bits
of work, scraps of conversation,
crumbs to keep him connected.
Young, quiet, from up North.
That's all we ever knew of him.

Come autumn we're sharing cider
in Holywell. Out there in Cornmarket
the pickings from bins are meagre now
the last coaches withdraw for the season;
leaves are crisped by first frost; names
here are chiselled, rimed white,
distinguished, remembered.

They told us they found him overdosed
alone by the water. Even death
it seems has degrees and mansions.
Here's no site to visit, just another
nameless unfortunate like us,
another unmarked burial.

The November sky eyelid slides
shut over the council offices
over the Job Centre and colleges.
Dark bites into our bones.

HELEN KIDD

Paper Houses

Dark is almost on the loose tonight,
streets of shadows walking as men.
Behind curtained windows, lights are dim.
At a desk at a drawing behind the bars

of one upper storey, someone is working.
While the warm and populated night
slips softly by him, he is making paper
houses: fold-out, pop-up, slim town-houses.

The floor is littered, the walls are lined
with them. The ones on the mantelpiece
are torch-lit from within. They are high
and buoyant as light-ships. Behind them

in the mirror the room reflects dimly;
there are some houses, and a man, working.
The night flows on beneath him.
The walls of the house are paper-thin.

JANE GRIFFITHS

Oxford Rewley

Grandpont Carfax from his temple cowley
with his ashmolean dragons cool
came headington the iffley horspath,
his brasenose bodleian the botley crew.

He's godstow hinksey in holywell keble,
his balliol osney with magdalen.
He's cumnor court the Hertford Linacre,
her isis oriel in sheldonian green.

But Jericho Bartlemas in his ruskin wolvercote
came wadham wytham the parks,
and on Deadman's Walk he shotover Grandpont
and pembroke him nuffield in the pitt-rivers ebbes.

The high, the broad, the plain and the littlemore
are merton and marston to the castle mound
to cherwell Jericho and the Hertford Linacre;
'tis somerville binsey now, 'tis summertown.

Grandpont Carfax from his temple cowley
with his ashmolean dragons cool
came headington the iffley horspath,
his brasenose bodleian the botley crew.

BOB COCKBURN

St Clement's Church

Irrefutable as every winter
The church still stands in the city's hinterland,
Black, blockish and Norman through bare branches.

An evening moon turns slowly in the sky
While blackbirds blink among the several graves
And ivy twines the shadows into darkness.

Bleak and miraculous this winter hour
Is the church, the cadence of its gables,
The dark account of its massive tower.

I step back, amazed as an artist
By the nave's Byzantine arches,
By the ages that the stone so starkly houses.

Shall I rejoice or grieve this evening
That the nearest I have felt to grief
Is caused by this: the cold clear light,

The fit of stone on stone so tight
You could not slip a knife, a blade of grass
Between them, split the clasp of centuries?

ROBERT MACFARLANE

Between the Balls

Oxford is a two-faced city,
a charming liar
an old-world demi-monde
fashioned from indecent piety
by white upper-class men
to satisfy their dreaming spires;
(a rich kid lathering to meet
his parents' expectations,
the gargoyle intellectual
with a heart of cotswold stone).

Her eyes flash £ signs
as she raises her skirts
to tourist buses,
sips champagne at a Merton ball,
sucks up to the well-off and venal,
fleeces visitors to Magdalen hall.
Her red light is the pink blush
of too much beer on Saturday nights;
her postcard is the punt
poled up the river at dawn.

Most of what she earns
is swallowed by college pimps,
leaving her hungrier
than Isis ducks in winter,
homeless, probably drunk,
snoring in the doorway
of Barclays Bank or
tugging trouser-legs for pence
to feed her baby
outside the Quaker Meeting House
after the last bike has been nicked.

SUE SHAW

Oxford

This morning I pass a big clump of purple buddleia
by the river and catch their honeyed scent
and notice again how they're shaped like *kulfi*
– like Indian icecream
then as I walk towards the Bodleian
there's this old man finishing a yellow dream-
like enormous watercolour of the Radcliffe
Camera – perhaps he's a nephew
of Charles Ryder? with that precious nostalgia
which might be all this cavalier place is meant
to mean though take that word *camera*
and you'll find it means *room* in Latin
just as the word *kamra* in Punjabi
also means *room*
so that from the Land of the Five Rivers
to Ancient Rome
to this three hundred year and more dome
is as short and sweet as a piece of *burfi*

TOM PAULIN

Feller, Son & Daughter

The child has never seen before
how big the farmyard creatures are:
he meets a pig's man-size,
appeasing stare, opens his mouth
to the unquacking duck, reaches out
a mittened paw to touch the gash
in the deer's dark fur. It's arched,
mid-leap, but with its head
and hooves cut off. He wants

to ask, but it's their turn, at last,
and Feller's man must check their chit,
and hook the Christmas turkey
down. He's bloodstained, expert,
kind. He tucks the bird
behind the pram, duveted in wax paper,
straps the wee boy snug in front,
grins, makes him a crown
of butcher's grass and holly.

The child shakes his fists and sings,
all the way home, the five gold rings,
chants to impervious feet
on shining streets, his list of lords,
french hens, and swans. It is
a litany of the near-extinct: beasts
known by name and husbanded,
birds falconed down, or shot and hung,
all butchered, paid, accounted for.

Kate Clanchy

Shafting the Kids

a love story set in the 1980s

Merrydown diddle, whiskey-fingered fiddle and
my guy jumped out the New Inn. This little slag
laughed to see such fun 'cause there was no need
to ask what he'd been up to. This little slag laughed
as the shirt tails fluttered over moonlit buttocks
of Cowley Road fuckers. And, if his new slag needs
a good shafting tonight, why not do it in the road?
It's hard to say goodnight politely when you're sitting
on somebody's face; the fact that new slag managed it
at all only adds, "Hah, Hah," to the pain on my face.
"Shafting Tonight" might erect in neon above
like the Lionel's Tattoo Studio sign we admired
from the bus' top deck when I still had a smile
on my face; when we used to come all over the place;
but back to the slag's tail although my guy never left it.

Her seduction of my nice man was once all the story
that interested me; and the main point, did she really
give him more and bigger stiffies? But, seeing them at it
on the roadside, I can't help wondering if there's
something more to it all inside? Why did he let her take
the steering wheel? Broom, broom, what a nice, nice man.

New Slag and Nice Guy self-styled East Oxford Anarchists:
because they make a lot of money and they don't care
how they earn it. "Hah, Hah" in the bar: they didn't see me
over the top of their suit collars. One of their hobbies
is picking up cats from Brett's burnt-out burger stall
and skinning them for laboratories. "A tenner a time."
Cat suits make a comeback. Didn't you wonder
why? These kids are hard. And the Slag and Nice Guy,
"Well, we often live together for convenience".
"Hah, Hah." Waiting on the day they can plan, negotiate,
wheel-deal, finance, settle, legal-document, sellotape,
wall-tight, vacuum, sandwich, cress-and-crap glad-wrap
their mortgages. And then tax-deduct them.
Basically these kids are shite.

But this is a love story. My name's Mary and we were
just ordinary until he got that job with the city council.
I played my part – just followed the bus route
from the dole alone now to the Swan, made good lasagne
and listened. He was well-paid in the poll-tax brigades:
twenty an hour easy and free black Levis. And that's
where he met that rich slag, so no job fetches no
nice guy: now what could have gone wrong?

But back to the street sex scene: kids of shame.
Shafting slags. No need to sound like a tabloid
because they'll come in a minute. Just time to explain,
when money is easy and you're on the law's right side
with full permission to take people's homes to bits –
bit by bit: street-shagging is the only solution
for some fun. All the danger, the need for perfect timing,
and the thrill of high-performance joy-riding:
guaranteed crowd-pleaser, and real cop-teaser.
Trained to be fuckers from the day we're born, m'lud.
"Hah, Hah."
And the better the shafting – the louder the applause.

But back to the street sex scene. Central TV coming in
for the big-cock angle. But the news team got uptight
about the anti-Nonnie Tiffany and other civic dignitary graffiti.
Dipped-out bastards. Shifting the cameras to avoid the dirty bits.
No politics. Just lots of tits. They want trancing in ravehouse,
funk-punk, drug-parties-pens/prisons kids, too dipped-out-yoof,
to fuck anybody up. "Our reporter penetrated drugs parties/
kids scene. And he gave them a jolly good shafting."

They want the Slag and Mr. Nice Guy fondling in ecstasy:
too dumb to see an icon when I can:
but this is a love story.

I can aspire to something higher than a nice man's cock;
well, call me an Anarchist and watch me,
instead of jumping under the no. 52, I'll start my own shafting.
I got off Cowley Shag-Pile Carpet Road, got onto
the accommodating driver's seat and ran down the whole row
of pricks. The lovers. The cameras. The crowd.
Like a row of the littlest pebbles. A slight discomfort
to my genitals: that old Deep-Heat rub feel.
It made second feature on the local news.

Basically these kids were meant to be passed over
– all the papers just screamed sex crimes –
with only a minor hiccup. And, although the screaming
got quite loud, no questions were asked in the House.
And there were no complaints.

P.S. – I have in fact received some complaints since writing
"Shafting the Kids", from the Oxford City Council, the Oxford Times,
the Inspector Morse Tourist Trail Development Agency, Central
Television, the Alhambra Lane Residents Association, etc. These I feel
obliged to record in spite of having my name cleared in a court of law
of any guilt with regard to my alleged crime.
    Thank you however to the Bullingdon regulars and the Leys
Automobile Enthusiasts Club for their unstinting support.

BRIDGET HOBBS

Patio Breakfast

At last warm enough to be outside.
A surprising trio round your rusty table
munching muesli and left-over strawberries –
us, still in the early stages,
and a Buddhist nun in a burgundy robe
being uncompassionate to the croissants.
I kept looking over my shoulder.
The garden seemed an image of you,
run slightly wild yet beautiful.
Behind the housetops I imagined
crossing the bridge to reach the colleges.
I couldn't have plotted any course
to lead me to this time and place.
Yet here somehow I was, ready to admit
to an unaccustomed feeling.
That was why I looked over my shoulder
checking that this wasn't a dream,
this strange Sunday morning compote –
you, me, and a nun in burgundy
at breakfast in an Oxford garden.

BRIAN LEVISON

St Michael at the North Gate

Saxon. A lone survivor. The tower
leans against clouds, honey on grey.
Lifts from the particle-accelerator

of the crowds. Above the heave,
huge bells. A peal of six-mouth silence.
Centuries hang in the untongued air.

Inside, the cool sheets your skin.
Sapphire and scarlet shale
through stained glass. Edge an angel.

The snail of the stairs coils upwards.
Lancet windows: needles of light.
A space to pause. Peer out. Like a monk.

You reach the top. Panoramas of roofs.
Crenellations of pigeons. See the sun's
finger on the braille of the hills.

Far below, your other self
still chases through the labyrinth,
pinned to shopping lists, pavement thoughts.

LYNNE WYCHERLEY

Looking for My Mother in Blackwell's

for Joan Emmitt (1929–1992)

If I search long enough
I know I will find you here
in your worn leather jacket,
wedged between Eliot and Pound
or sidling up to Plath
hunched over slim volumes
peeling back the pages. Hungry.

It's your idea of heaven
the well-stocked shelves
the aisles of wordy packages –

I won't find you among the cookbooks
or in the lush green and mottled frenzy
of the gardening section, or in family health,
but with your face deep in Woolf,
stalking the corridors of fiction
like a frantic tiger.

I will recognize
the lean slant of your back,
the way you pushed your glasses
to the end of your nose to read,
as if the words were a map,
and you the traveller.

I could never travel as you did,
weightless, unencumbered.
I've packed my books, you'd say,
a pair of jeans and a notebook.
I'll be in touch.

    I'll be in touch.

MARTA EMMITT

An Oxford Academic is Confused

I'm reading the life of Madame de Staël
partly so, when Oxford academics at cocktail parties
ask me what I'm reading, I can say:
I'm reading the life of Madame de Staël.

I'm reading a book about Wittgenstein, I say,
careful to pronounce the W like a V.
They narrow their eyes and rummage
in their minds for obscure facts
about his love of celery or hatred of dogs.

Wasn't it strange about his love of celery?
they ask (in Latin),
then take a swift about-turn and scurry
over some tenuous bridge that links
Wittgenstein to their own subject.
Of course, Rilke also had a love of celery,
perhaps this has a bearing on deconstruction...

They smile kindly but firmly at my hemline
thinking they have routed me. But I am wising up.
I beat a swift retreat back to Madame de Staël, asking:
Do we know if Madame de Staël liked celery?

While they ponder this, I console myself
thinking: well, I have cleared up a whole house today
plus replacing the toilet rolls in both lavatories –
never mind Rilke.

jennyklewis@gmail.com

If only a Marilyn with the brain of Einstein
could turn up in her Wonderbra
and stump the bastards.
It would be worth the whole of history
to be there for that brief moment
when a question is asked, a silence falls,
a sherry glass twirls nervously – and

an Oxford academic is confused.

JENNY LEWIS

with love from
Jenny (Lewis!)
xx

the first frisbee of spring

this morn i awoke
to the hum of the song
of the first frisbee of spring
calling me forth
from duveted slumber
– down dusty stairs
overstepping the morning's tight-lipped manila'd mail
and out, out into the morning air
chilled and warmed and charming

across Rymers Lane she called me
Saturday's sunlazy carstrewn streets
through Florence Park's damp dewy budding splendour
wet with promise and
gently steaming with earthy sighs

past Larkrise School hollow and childless
along two sides of the Boundary Brook Road
fluttering past the bookies on Howard Street she flew

in and out of sun and shade and sun
air chilled and charmed and warming
my body hairs bristled in her wake
– bristling through the icy pockets of night-time air
bristling with a wintered but now waking joy
over and along the Iffley Road
and down, down the welcome riverward roll of Jackdaw Lane
to the tufted bumpety football pitches of Meadow Lane
i followed her sound and song

and there
in the cool valleyed lowlands of east oxford
i caught my first glimpse
of the first frisbee of spring
hovering above the penalty box
dervish and steady and strong
she rose and then she fell
in glorious spinning murmur

STEPHEN HANCOCK

Lampblack

Tudor and coarse, like a stuck pig, the story
runs through these raked-over streets
to a darkened stone grid. Though Oxford's
no Venice, with its keel barnacled by plaques
and inscriptions, we've plenty enough:
the Leveller soldiers in Gloucester Green,
the aeronaut's field, Hooke's laboratory
and these grim-faced cobbles, smoothed
by the river of a hundred thousand days.

Cycling down Broad Street,
my first full day here (mistakenly thinking
it runs north to south) and my front wheel
jars, a turned ankle, slotting into
a stone hot-cross-bun in the middle of the road,
bucks handlebars, stumbles me into
a parking-ticket box. Cranmer, I think;
Latimer, Ridley, now me. Martyrs all,
on a plain cross for the degraded priests.

Soot, that is the echo of a lantern.
X marks the spot. It is happening here,
the burning of a faction.
Like pork, you would think, but they are old men
and not sausages, all is grease and smoke
from the faggots of wood dragged up the Broad,
built into a tar-soaked haystack
against the slight, unceasing rain of a March dawn.
I renounce Cranmer's Oxford,

My pale beliefs have less substance than the crows
among shuttered clerestories
of all the deconsecrate houses of God
in Jericho. I renounce these whispers
of echoes rolling like skulls down old streets,
the streets in their tangled ball of string
that tightens to twine or coarsens to hemp
and is frayed in parts, and is burned.
I would chisel the stones out, and plant there a tree.

GRAHAM NELSON

Fake

– you say, and shed your fur across the chair.
As if you would, as if you'd touch 'the real beast' –
what is it these people take you for? And this,
a coat from your father, having days before
measured his length beside the church:
a broken toe, a key-hole bruise of a nose.

A hundred miles and two turns up the Thames
punts jigger as we giggle out
to the far boats and slip the knot
nudging each one off
like cattle we're sending home.

He's slowing down, you say, *my father*.
Though frankly I was enjoying the picture
of a single punt stealing downriver
for the Watermans Reach, the Folly Bridge

and out for some black shire field,
where a fake fox stops at a head-wind
chased by fake hounds.

<small>MATTHEW HOLLIS</small>

Trickle-Down Effect

She spins and hums
in hot metallic
pigeon-winged air
with shoppers
and scholars,
mad as a gnat
dizzy from rolling
with too many punches.
In our wasp-trap city
she acts out for all
us nine-to-fivers
lifts ragged skirts
and pisses
copious, eloquent,
over the shocked windows
of the Alliance & Leicester.

HELEN KIDD

Hollow Centre

Long lines of buses wait
Under cold october's rain
Under their umbrellas go
All the well-fed ladies so

The monument reads 1897
R.I.P. to the men who died
The drunks lie beneath
Heads bare in the rain

Sleek black boy waits
For his thin white girl
He keeps the needle
She'll use it again

The stench of diesel
Keeps low to the ground
And the beggars look bored
Now the tourists have gone

A lone piper plays
Outside Marks & Spencer's
His suitcase lies open
To catch coins in the rain

The notes that he plays
Drift like smoke in the night
Amazing grace
Like a bird on the wing

Love don't pay the rent
And there's five months of winter
The out of town bus
Appears thru the rain

MAURICE O'CONNOR

Streetsurfing

There are some
with their names in stars
on the street
with a little talent
and a little luck.

There are many
with no name
on the streets
with a lot more talent
and a lot less luck.

JAMES WISE

The Saxon Pin

Under the fortress mound a Saxon cloak-pin waits.

Protected also by the pit they threw him in
it will not soon be found.
But silver can endure
past centuries of idle change.

Next door, a second Norman castle rots
into an English gaol
where cells are painted yellow
to match the contents of the plastic chamber-pots.
A stony yard encumbers exercise,
and slowly, serving sentence after sentence,
the graceless uniforms wear thin.

The mound matures more kindly.
Couples climb up to learn their business,
shaking out hair like smoke
above the clanking of the shunting-yards.
Later they like to feel each other's way
with candle pieces
down the crumbling, littered steps
that bring them briefly home within its buried well-head.

The long divergent lovers will not see
the sun explode,
the prison vaporize, the mound dissolve,
nor, picoseconds after those,
the Saxon pin.

RIP BULKELEY

Early November Takes Shape

In the shopping walkways, vast green cones
with ragged edges, hung with huge gold bows
have ousted, overnight, squashed orange orbs,
small black cones and silhouettes of webs.

Now a plump brown sphere with darker blobs
and cream paint dribbled on its far-up top
round spikes of green, sits in a fluffy off-white
swathe. Music jangles from inside.

Shreds of threaded aluminium dangle
overhead, held to the roof with spangly
stars, and slung between the shops are winking
coloured bulbs, illuminating nothing.

What month should I return for cubes of red,
blue cylinders and purple pyramids?

RACHEL WIGGANS

A View of Oxford

Where a hoof-print in the lower, right-hand margin
of a moonlit page is not, after all,
some cunning gin
or pit-fall

or little trip-wire
whereby a don
might connect the bard in the booley-byre
with *boustrophedon*

but itself a footnote, itself a gloss
on a passage of cattle, their muddling through a place
that, even in Hilary,

is bordered by Queen Anne's Lace
and fritillary that tends towards fritillary
as loss tends towards loss.

Paul Muldoon

At the Martyrs' Memorial

We hoist our sail – an old sheet – and sit down.
VIGIL, it tells the incurious passers-by,
FOR NAGASAKI AND HIROSHIMA.

I never really liked this crusted spike
reminder of the old intolerance
on the stained steps of which pissed yobs have pissed
and derelicts have drunk and vomited
so what the devil am I doing here?

City men dressed in suits and self-importance,
women whose breast-milk must be UHT,
respectable burghers who avert their eyes,
lovers whose eyes are only for themselves.

"I'll come and join you for a little while",
a young man says, and sits down quietly.

An eminent scholar whom I happen to have
nodding acquaintance with – my pulse goes up –
passes without a flicker. *Demonstrations,*
vulgar even to seem to notice them.
And one doesn't expect to see people one knows.

Two waitresses watch from the big hotel
hoping we'll do something remarkable
or get arrested, or get beaten up.

Three *rather prosperous-looking* Irish, begging.

Four punks. "I'm for the bomb", one says; only his mate
has PROTEST AND SURVIVE in silver studs.
A third turns round and bares his bum at us.

Some men shout from a car. Their words are drowned
by traffic noise, but we can read their views
in their fierce faces and up-jabbing fingers.

Afraid of anger and afraid of pain
this human wash would have me overboard
if my companions weren't such doughty sailors.

Dust in our eyes, lead in our lungs, fumes, din,
a hard shell hiding the soft earth from us...
I caught a feather as it floated past,
and once a blackbird skimmed a double-decker.
A single duck flies over, heading east,
bound for some grassy eyot in the river.
I look for comfort at the leaves of plane-trees,
those and the live gold edging of the clouds,
that and the blue sky deepening to evening,
deepening to a glowing cornflower night.

I think of Cranmer, loath to die for dogma,
only they said they'd burn him all the same,
who reaffirmed the things that he believed in
and died, his right hand blazing first, in fervour.
Author of peace his collect had us pray,
three centuries of morning congregations,
so certain who *our adversaries* were.

KIM TAPLIN

OX4, Oxford

for Leander

Good bye OX4, Oxford. I liked you.
The people I met through you.
Too many drugs on the Cowley Road
they say. I didn't see much but a few pills
and yes, stuff to smoke that makes you write
silly things in loop, silly things in loop indeed
but when you're writing them you are God,
like a nerd playing SimCity, yet

taking that, there was no day after,
that's all.

Good bye OX4, Oxford. I will miss you.
The people I met through you.
My friend Syrithe on the other side of the Cowley
eating veggie and making delicious herbal tea,
my green neighbours recycling whatever
they could in their garden, the fish'n'chips guy
from Iran who said "my friend" to everyone
and worked twelve hours a day with a smile,
my grocer from Pakistan asking me about Paris
spending all his money for the kiddies in EuroDisney,

and the girl from the other side of Iffley Road
who had stoned blue eyes, for she always was,
and dyed her hair red like the deepest of sins.
My Salomé from East Oxford. How I lost my head, yet

having her, there was no day after,
that's all

there is to say, that's all.
Good bye OX4, Oxford, good bye.

LUCILE DESLIGNÈRES

Another Day

Waking with the thud on my chest
of a hungry cat and the thud on my head
of a thirsty night, I look long and hard
at the cracks in the ceiling and
turn back to find my
dreamworld.

Gone. As clean as the toilet
after the cold flush of morning.
My memory gathers the pieces
of yesterday's tomorrow
dropped in haste
with the first
slug last
night.

Picking up the debris
of last night's abandonment,
I sink into the bathwater,
let the muck float off my skin.
I re-emerge re-covered
and ready.

SALLY HORSMAN

Twenty Lengths

Today I am uneasy in the water,
the strokes do not come smoothly.

My daily metamorphosis
from pachyderm to crocodile to

water-snake has failed. The water
eddies, stalls on unseen lumps.

I don't know why. I lumber, twist
onto my back and smell the pine trees.

I gaze at the greys of clouds and wonder
why I cannot slither sinuously like yesterday.

Perhaps a breeze has made the water
harder. Sent the ripples crossways.

And then a wall of water thumps my head.
I turn and see a man churn furious

lengths as if his life's ambition
is fracturing the upturned sky, thrashing

waves to all the edges of the world.
I wonder how his fury feels

and what it's like to make the biggest splash.
Then he leaves and I slide quietly into fish.

RACHEL WIGGANS

"A View Over Flat Country"

I did not seek it.
I came in out of the rain,
set down my shopping,
and sank thankfully
onto a nearby seat,

and looked up to see,
in a faded gilded frame,
an immense landscape
simply entitled
"A View Over Flat Country".

Such a sense of space,
of a prospect reaching out
beyond the confines
of canvas, making
the frame quite arbitrary.

A long line of light
defines the far horizon;
yet the dazzle hides
the precise limit
of that level stretch of land.

Fainter haloes glow
round the crowns of high-piled clouds.
Below, the shady plain
is striated by
the sheen of distant rivers.

Little by little
my eyes settle on details –
clustered cottages,
a coach and horses,
people talking at a door –

but always return
to that elusive skyline,
its tantalizing
luminosity,
its reach towards the infinite.

BERYL HAIGH

Finding Out

A small girl stares
with her nose
against the glass
at the dried-up heads
hung on strings
a tribe child slung by a hook
in his hair

She stands rooted there

At the base of the case
something lies
wrapped up in layers

Paper thin
disintegrating

She wants very much
to look away
but her eyes have to know
if what is lying
inside the shroud
has a face a finger
a proper set of toes

The attendant knows

Opening the door of the case
he watches her face
as he pulls back the dress
as far as the feet

Tiny
blackened
almost complete

TINKER MATHER

Home-Thoughts

with apologies to Robert Browning

Thank goodness I'm in Oxford,
Now that April's here
And whoever wakes in Oxford
Sees, some morning, unaware,
That prunus and forsythia bear a sudden load
Of pink and yellow blossom all down the Banbury Road
And they are mightily relieved they do not live in Slough –
But in Oxford – now!

And after April, when May follows,
Morrells pubs will be full of thirsty swallows!
While the finch's song and the thrush's trills
Will be drowned by the ringing of Blackwell's tills
Where flocks of tourists twitter as they buy
Their city guides before they mob the Broad and High.

Hark, as the shabby undergraduate bemoans
His anorexia induced by student loans,
A well-connected girl with dimpled knees
Is giving rickshaw rides to smiling Japanese,
And starving waifs in St Ebbes doorways hunch
While ladies meet at Debenhams for *Slimmer's Lunch*.

And though from Blackbird Leys to Summertown
The blooms, from traffic fumes, are tinged with brown;
Though jobs are scarce from Marston and Rose Hill
To Headington and Cowley Road, I still
Can't help but pity those in York or Crewe
Whose skies are not enhanced by Oxford blue.

Jenny Lewis

Lunchbreak in the City, with Pigeon

Half an hour outside
of blanket noonday heat,
and lavender, gloom blue,
weighed down with bees.
Tortoiseshells,
tossed bus-tickets,
flitter, alight.
Grass dries to straw.
Faint floribundas topple.
Somewhere above the roar
a feathered matriarch claps:
"Your time's up, dearie!
Your time's up, dearie!
Your time's up!"

GINA WILSON

* Site of the King's House, birthplace of Richard I,
  'Cœur de Lion', in 1157.

New Year's Eve

Even in the village the pubs are packed.
The din drives us out again, into the night.
And the night is still mild, welcoming.

We walk on past quiet houses,
secretive behind their lighted windows,
and take the path to the weir

where the water somersaults.
I let the white noise rush through my head,
glad for now not to hear our footsteps.

Across the widest stretch of the river
mysterious cows, moonlight on their flanks,
bunch at the water's edge.

And the river is in full spate. Although we seem
to be walking against the flow
the current is pulling us fast downstream.

I am trying to trust it. Somewhere in the distance
fireworks scatter pink and gold
briefly above rooftops. It must be midnight.

And I could stay here watching the river
but we come back up to street level
and tramp the last half-mile

full-circle past the Co-op, go inside,
light the fire and crack a bottle,
toast the new year in.

<small>WENDY DAVIES</small>

Hinksey

o the flatness of Hinksey
is lovelier than mountains
when the moon beams through the pylons
and mallards skim the lake

from the bridge across the sidings
this sweet and soft spring evening
and down the Devil's Backbone
where the blackthorn wears white blossoms

over gravel and alluvium
to the stile where some boys shared their cider with me
there's a lull in the dual carriageway
you can hear the big band rehearsing
and New Hinksey folk going to the General Elliott
greet South Hinksey folk on their way to the Seven Stars

EDWARD POPE

Drake

Only a clockwork toy could go so wrong.
But the drake is going, his balance gone, his motor
stuck on spin, on overdrive. Twisting
over the water in dislocated spurts
he is driven in punishing circles in a chase for his
curling tail. However many snaps
he takes he never gets to bite it. He struggles,
half in, half out of the water, a rag duck, dunked
and slapped on an underwater stone.

A moorhen comes to look and backs away.

Shamed into making a good display, even if
it's the last, he rears up like a cobra,
striking at spectres, green head caught in the sun,
before being ironed out by the wind, one wing
splayed onto the grey sheet of the water.

Sucked into the flood of diluted mud he is slowly
going under. Button eye, nut-brown breast
go down with his wishing bone. The water closing
over covers the curl of his tail. Concentric
rings, empty as evening, fan out towards
the moorhen. She thinks it is the end. But up
he comes, thrown up by the water one last time,
to lay his head on the river, sideways down.

TINKER MATHER

Sketch

In a café basement, off the kitchen
sitting up in a light-well, is a wire sculpture
a slender woman, her steely fingers
splayed, pushed against the glass as if she knows
not me but everyone I could be.

So I should note the look on her face as tense
and wary as I am, curious to know
these hard lines and what to read between them.
She is a model's study of the artist
though it isn't me she would catch exactly.

A waitress raises the pad in her palm
as if a still-life of apples in a bowl
was there to render quickly in soft lead.
What if she could offer the cross-hatched fruit
to the overcast breezed-through chicken-wired

figure whose blood-line would carry a fence-pulse?
The world upstairs is calling in the light.
Below the street she alone has caught the sun:
a brightening filament, an optimist
in the summer when her glass door is opened

and oven-heat escapes, her transparent hope
an after-image etched on air for as long
as we can draw breath, our anticipation
pencilled in. The waitress who walks through the swing-door
will not be the one who comes back.

GREG SWEETNAM

Convent of the Sacred Heart

Many have knelt here long and so they say
this room is full of prayer, a soft and lachrymal
suffusion to sparge dim, weary seekers.

And yet, today, this room is full of sun
and all the windows shine with rose magnolia,
spinning bone-china cups along wry boughs
where squint-tailed squirrels perch as, down below,
the April-waking snail re-slimes his track.

And, in this room, I swear I hear a high
ripieno of pappaluffeling flutes, light
as seeds of cotton-grass afloat on morning air.

GINA WILSON

Sunset over Port Meadow

I watched the sun roll
down the nape of the hill
like a great ball caught by Atlas.

I watched the most perfect gold coin
fall from a careless palm
into nothingness, and all the people

seemed to be standing in rags
at the edge of a biblical flood.
But to the girls on bikes

dodging the rocks in the path and laughing,
to the beautiful girl with
sandstone lips and a terrier called Max,

to the couples with their children,
the dropping of the sun
like the corner of space melting

was nothing to be remarked on;
no more than if you
had looked up from among the swans,

and when I did not move
had crossed the bridge towards me.
Mothers running to their daughters

are a commonplace, and the sun of
unimaginable red, rolling away
and turning the water to death

and the grass to flesh,
leaving the world with no promises,
is a commonplace.

POLLY CLARK

Nocturne

Through that many-windowed room,

Northside street-lamps show in the southside firs
Like stage lights casting a small ballet of branches.

There must be difficult laws of light,
Perspective, and so on, operating here.

She would ask some Optics person, soon.

Meanwhile her book, her fire, her tea,
The sense that her eyes, looking so long,
Had begun to see.

AVRIL BRUTEN

Dear Catharine,

Today I passed (already past again, before the hour
is fully saved or savoured) that house. Home
more years and selves than we should now remember.
Its face unchanged
– a few skins of brick-dust thinner;
the gallant quince more gaunt. Around the corner,
grey in a gaudy bus, a woman rode
you too would have forgotten.
Fine, I thought
(sentimental as an unfaithful love),
the soft persistency of roots and flowers.
It is spring, and where are we? who made the place
our theatre, bower, confidante; our other
parent. I should like to think
our ghosts were happy. And if only
you were here to raid the costume box
for your old tight-fitting shadow and surprise
once more the single self that looked
so many years from our four eyes …

I recall
one summer day, a lady standing here –
old; blind; corrugate as a shell.
She asked: Was this house number twenty?
Where are the wall and ornamental railings?
Is there a lawn? A lilac tree?
She had lived here in the war. And I remember,
answering her questions, steering
across the yard, how utterly
her past did not belong here any more.

TERESA MORGAN

oxfordisney

following the umbrella they listen
to Morse signals on
personal stereos. They imbibe

the genuine ale of unreality,
the scent of dusty jackets
in room-lined shelves, the cough

of pure erudition. It is sexless,
like a child's step through
the looking-glass, a timeless

ever-never. If people are born
here they bear no weight.
The dead breathe, speak

volumes. The umbrella shades
the curious from the banal
light of decay. Magdalen's

crisp clean tower once smudged
the horizon over
Christ Church meadow, and

in the Bodleian books ache
with the burden
of old thought, old sex.

Reality laser-bombs the quads
but hits the hospital,
the sleeping-bagged shadows

in doorways. "In this
study a middle-aged don
teaches a young lady

the passions of Jude."

KEITH JEBB

Fine

"How are you?"

Socket-eyed milestone (must've had a plate or plaque
    attached to it, bolted on the front).
Soft, slow 'whoosh, whoosh, whoosh'
    growing louder behind me,
    over right shoulder,
    along canal.
Getting nearer, getting louder.
A swan!, and another!, and another!,
Gods they're big!
So lazily and effortlessly flying past,
    necks outstretched,
Wings slowly, languorously beating
    (could break a man's leg, those wings).

But not today.

The first, white, under and through the bridge.
    Second, brown and white mottled,
    banking to port and climbing, and over.
    Third, brown and white, and through.
Whoosh! Whoosh! Whoosh!
How regretfully boring, predictable and prosaic
    the sun on the red, yellow, golden leaves had seemed.

Sorry? Fine.

BOB WEEDON

Cardiopathy

It was as if a pigeon had been trapped,
fallen from its chimney perch
half-starved behind the mantel –
wings flailing against the brick
setting an avalanche of twigs
and grit, gobbets of dry bread,
crumbling mortar, clots of soot,
feathers adrift, the frightened tremor
of its inner movement revealed
through the resonance of the wall –
a faint coo-coo, dying to be heard.

STEPHEN WILSON

* Cardiac Ward

On Seeing Tom Paulin in B & Q

What would tempt a poet out of
the Venice of the South Midlands
up here to where the Cowley Road
meets the Oxford Road coming back?

Only the indigenous poets of this great
cathedral to self-sufficiency the men
from the five villages that died on the
buddy system great with each other in
wars too great for them. A kind of glory
in it to die so burred and unbelieving
all their rounded edges rounded still.

Rosaleen Croghan

The Almond Tree

I

All the way to the hospital
the lights were green as peppermints.
Trees of black iron broke into leaf
ahead of me, as if
I were the lucky prince
in an enchanted wood
summoning summer with my whistle,
banishing winter with a nod.

Swung by the road from bend to bend,
I was aware that blood was running
down through the delta of my wrist
and under arches
of bright bone. Centuries,
continents it had crossed;
from an undisclosed beginning
spiralling to an unmapped end.

II

Crossing (at sixty) Magdalen Bridge
Let it be a son, a son, said
the man in the driving mirror,
Let it be a son. The tower
held up its hand: the college
bells shook their blessing on his head.

III
I parked in an almond's
shadow blossom, for the tree
was waving, waving me
upstairs with a child's hands.

IV
Up
the spinal stair
and at the top
along
a bone-white corridor
the blood tide swung
me swung me to a room
whose walls shuddered
with the shuddering womb.
Under the sheet
wave after wave, wave
after wave beat
on the bone coast, bringing
ashore – whom?
                    New-
minted, my bright farthing!
Coined by our love, stamped with
our images, how you
enrich us! Both
you make one. Welcome
to your white sheet,
my best poem!

V

At seven-thirty
the visitors' bell
scissored the calm
of the corridors.
The doctor walked with me
to the slicing doors.
His hand upon my arm,
his voice – *I have to tell
you* – set another bell
beating in my head:
your son is a mongol
the doctor said.

VI

How easily the word went in –
clean as a bullet
leaving no mark on the skin,
stopping the heart within it.

This was my first death.
The '*I*' ascending on a slow
last thermal breath
studied the man below

as a pilot treading air might
the buckled shell of his plane –
boot, glove, and helmet
feeling no pain

from the snapped wires' radiant ends.
Looking down from a thousand feet
I held four walls in the lens
of an eye; wall, window, the street

a torrent of windscreens, my own
car under its almond tree,
and the almond waving me down.
I wrestled against gravity,

but light was melting and the gulf
cracked open. Unfamiliar
the body of my late self
I carried to the car.

VII

The hospital – its heavy freight
lashed down ship-shape ward over ward –
steamed into night with some on board
soon to be lost if the desperate

charts were known. Others would come
altered to land or find the land
altered. At their voyage's end
some would be added to, some

diminished. In a numbered cot
my son sailed from me; never to come
ashore into my kingdom
speaking my language. Better not

look that way. The almond tree
was beautiful in labour. Blood-
dark, quickening, bud after bud
split, flower after flower shook free.

On the darkening wind a pale
face floated. Out of reach. Only when
the buds, all the buds, were broken
would the tree be in full sail.

In labour the tree was becoming
itself. I, too, rooted in earth
and ringed by darkness, from the death
of myself saw myself blossoming,

wrenched from the caul of my thirty
years' growing, fathered by my son,
unkindly in a kind season
by love shattered and set free.

JON STALLWORTHY

The Temple Cowley Pool

Piggybacking my daughter,
water lenses the skin
of teenage girls glistening
at the full stretch of growth.

She is a camera. I don't even
have to press record.
What I see and she films
are two different scenes.

Dissolve from my cinemascopic
pan over the pool surface
(beach scene from Jaws)
to my goosefleshed arms at

one hundred erections per inch of skin,
POV a few inches above my head.
A perfect day unreels in the colour
of laughter, the giggles

that splash into words.
Action. Over and over, to her orders,
I perform this tableau:
she drowning, I hold her

above the chopping sharks.
After changing I know that
we'll sit on a particular table
and share a brand of crisps.

So the day is choreographed
until sleep's rushes spool
from her fingers, as she turns
and doggypaddles the duvet,

intent on the glow
pooling from water-stained lives,
editing all of that vision
to memory's jumpy feature.

GILES GOODLAND

Oxford Ireland

We gave it a total make-over: the tricolour
Over the Randolph and a big marquee
Given by the Rugby Club in exchange for the bar takings.
Christy Moore in the Town Hall and Dolores Keane
In the Randolph Ballroom, easily audible from
The commissionaired and private hotel garage.
All through a hot June weekend, it was Smithwicks
In plastic pints and barbecued sausages
And ice-cream, dancing and hurling and a tug o'war
With Irish teams from Headington and Deddington and Kirtlington.
Mothers lost children, just like Glounthane Sports
In the fifties, and found them skulking in the hot wind
From the generator and pulled them out leg-first.
Hard men tried to get in free, though otherwise
They didn't want to come at all. They'd pick a fight
With the sunburned stewards and threaten
To bring their brother. A two-mile tailback
Of Sunday traffic ("What the Hell's all this then?"),
It brought the tinkers from far and near, to give
Fivers to children after simple three-card tricks;
They crunched their hats in despair and screamed:
"Look at the size of him! We'll never stick it out, lads."
But they did. Reception from shook transistors
So fitful you hardly knew if Cork were winning.

You had to stay until the bitter end
In case you won the raffle and could carry off
A prize you didn't want triumphantly.
Monday – insubstantial pageant faded –
Back to normal; nothing left but a strip
Of salmon-pink tickets in your back pocket.

BERNARD O'DONOGHUE

Ox Carts at the Ford, *c.*1250

Thames – he had heard the name
as he walked this new land
after the rack of a sea voyage,
trudged tracks over chalk, slept
on the ground by a friar companion.

At the ford in a hill-rimmed bowl
of green, he takes a rest
where fritillaries lean to the winds,
and a blackbird chants from an oak.
Here is level land, easy to clear.

But soon a clatter of plates
will clash with bells that call
from chapels to study and prayer,
and feral choruses yell
to jolt him out of the scene,

an ugly sound of dispute
unlike philosophers' wrangle
or altercating divines.
Splatters of hate and blood
stain the rise of a city

until later a tower will build
shaped like those in his sunlit south,
another nearby, roofs, windows.
He hears plainsong challenge the bird.
Books arrive on ox carts

for libraries. Six million volumes
to stack above and below
a golden stone quadrangle. Windows
beam candlepower that illumines
each letter, page and hand.

The shout of the future fades
as he sinks into sounder sleep
and darkness enfolds him. The river
flows through his dream like learning,
runs on away and out of his time.

ANNE BORN

Avoiding the Cracks

I was walking along the path through the meadow
grass on one side, grass on the other
and the river at a distance

thinking desultorily of this and that
when I saw I was taking big steps and little steps
trying to avoid the cracks in the concrete.

Embarrassed, I put my foot down firmly
across a gaping fissure; then, whoosh! no warning
away went everything: my fine feather bed

my sturdy red bricks, the phone on the wall
the kitchen calendar, concepts of teatime
slipped through the gap like money through my fingers.

I wouldn't have minded going on that way
grass on one side, grass on the other
and the river at a distance

if it weren't for the children who appeared beside me
pulling at my hand, their mouths getting wider
threatening to drown me in their noisy darkness.

KATHLEEN MCPHILEMY

Night Bus to Blackbird Leys

On any Saturday night
you might find us
cruising among the ruins
lights on the dimmer
trying not to remember how
all that pollarded mirror
licking first began
boys and girls temporarily golden
foot down stampeding
most of us pissed
some of us on illegal medication
squashed pig-sick breathless
the Asian sub-continent tickled
up against a tiny foxy Scotsman
rock-rollicking round the Swan
careering on to Leys
hat-black greater and lesser
the undercarriage condescending
one wheel
and one wheel only.

ROSALEEN CROGHAN

BARNS ROAD

Botley Cathedral

Curved glass opacity
blank as a Kubrik monolith
a spire on top
like the RKO transmitter
placed there to reconcile
modernity with antiquity
and complement a famous
no longer somnolent view.

Situated due west
on clear evenings it catches
the sun's final light
then reflects it back east
in blinding gold and black tribute
to the colours of the city.

PAUL SUTTON

Port Meadow

Rosamund lay in Godstow walls;
My love, my royal love, she cried.
The abbess prayed and the winecup passed;
Wishes are horses and beggars ride.

A green-haired girl jumps down from her van,
A stud in her nose and a scar on her brow;
She runs with her dog and her dog with his fleas;
This place has never known the plough.

An archæologist stirs the mound,
Sifts the dust where the bronze man died,
Some ash and a bone and a twisted ring;
Wishes are horses and beggars ride.

Where Rosamund lay the birthwort grows;
The hummocked walls are crumbled now
And plastic picnics strew the grass;
This place has never known the plough.

Seven crows perch in a poplar tree,
Eleven swans on the river glide,
Green with nitrates, heavy with lead;
Wishes are horses and beggars ride.

Geese on the racetrack, ghosts at the lock,
Undieselled ghosts at the narrowboat's prow;
Wishes are horses and beggars ride,
This place has never known the plough.

MOLLIE CAIRD

The Legend of St Frideswide

How does sainthood fall
round the body of a girl,
the luminous folds
of a thousand projections?

Grey as an otter, she flees
to the bank. Burrs on her hem.
To where the angelic boatman burns,
his face like Antares.

At the ford, her pursuer
urges his horse. No date-rape
today: lightning stabs
like a holy proboscis,

blinding. Now his eyes
are craters in a pitted
moon-face and midnight
fills the chasm of his mouth.

Is she girl or goddess?
Pupating in her tree-ringed
oratory. Healing water
summoned by her voice.

Peasants and potentates
pressed at her shrine,
the Lionheart wading
through memories of blood.

For us, no angel on the river.
A swan for a star. As we pass,
almost pausing
at the mouth of her well

as if her hands could lift
these weights from our eyes.

Lynne Wycherley

Deep

Wild garlic throbs
in bluebell litter of leopard stipple
where aquamarine foliage
shafts nets of sunlight as if through water
lacing the shells
of last year's leaves
still crumbling and unresolved,

riffled by a thrush scavenging for worms.

Spiky tides of shoots
mirror in miniature
the masts of violet shadows soaring upwards
to tatter the sky
rattled by breezes that eddy and flow
rocking the crow's nest
of a creaking tree-top,
which shatters a branch and shivers the leaves
into mother of pearl
across the woodland floor.

SUE SHAW

from the halfway house

*for the detainees of Campsfield Immigration
Detention Centre, past present and future*

they give us the bureaucracy
of fact
         not the grasp of

in the foyer the empty vending machine
scrolls "have a nice
day" in blue lights

there are signs for standing
for smoking for fire escape
are things we do
in English.
               In Arabic, Lingala,
Yoruba we pass
time between us
               like a brown parcel

few days back the Algerians'
roof protest they
made the blood cross
on their chests
         to get read by

you say your papers
didn't print that?

and they were tippexed out of here

Keith Jebb

Leaving Oxford

You left a week before I did, and since
then Oxford hadn't been the same; a shift
of vision undeserved; I rinsed
the corners of my restless eyes, as if
there was a stiff disjunction there. The bus
turned down the High and crossed the bridge. I glimpsed
St Hilda's stony in the sun. The past
that Oxford stood for fell behind like dreams.
Once we were on the M40, there was
no space for tight manœuvre. You were home
and distant; tired, tense and terrified,
yet somewhere in the middle bound, I roamed
the country of emotions in a course
that wound from frontage to the pained inside.

HSIEN MIN TOH

In Oxford men don't
make love to you.

They give you some
typing to do.

Elsebeth Wulff

Rhyme

Sing a song of Oxford,
A skyline full of spires:
Four and twenty chiming;
All of them are liars.

All except for Christ Church,
Chiming past the hour:
A full five minutes later,
The voice of old Tom Tower.

I'd like to say to Christ Church
That Heaven's Greenwich timed,
And when the final trumpet sounds,
I'll be left behind.

J. M. BAILEY